METEORS

D0752213

The Truth Behind
Shooting Stars

METEORS

by Billy Aronson

A First Book

FRANKLIN WATTS

A DIVISION OF GROLIER PUBLISHING
New York ■ London ■ Hong Kong ■ Sydney
Danbury, Connecticut

Cover photograph ©: Photo Researchers (Pekka Parviainen/SPL)
Illustrations by MacArt Design

Photographs copyright ©: American Museum of Natural History: pp. 2, 44;
Bettmann Archive: pp. 18, 38, 47, 54; Comstock: p. 26; Hansen Planetarium:
p. 25 (Charles Capen); NASA: pp. 11, 12, 28, 49; National Museum of
Natural History, Smithsonian Institution: pp. 41, 52; Photo Researchers: pp.
8 (David Nunuk/SPL), 15 (Rev. Ronald Royer/SPL), 22 (Pearson and
Milon/SPL), 31 (Lynette Cook/SPL), 35 (Jerry Schad); Royal Observatory
Edinburgh: p. 29 (D. Malin); U.S.G.S. Photo Library, Denver, CO: p. 46 (Roddy
D.J.); UPI/Bettmann: p. 42

Library of Congress Cataloging-in-Publication Data

Aronson, Billy
Meteors: The truth behind shooting stars/ by Billy Aronson
p. cm. — (A First book)
Includes bibliographical references and index.
Summary: Explains such things as the difference between a meteor,
a meteoroid, and a meteorite and what happens when an asteroid
or comet gets too close to the earth.
ISBN 0-531-20242-9 (alk. paper)
1. Meteors—Juvenile literature. [1. Meteors.] I. Title. II. Series.
QB741.5.A76
523.5'1—dc20   95-48846
                                                                          CIP AC

© 1996 by Billy Aronson.
All rights reserved. Published simutaneously in Canada.
Printed in the United States of America.
1 2 3 4 5 6 7 8 9 10 R 05 04 03 02 01 00 99 98 97 96

CONTENTS

STARRY, STARRY NIGHT

CHAPTER 1

It's a clear, summer night. As you look up at the sky, you see thousands and thousands of bright, twinkling lights. You begin to wonder about the possibility of life on other planets. Each of the stars you see in the sky could be shining on other planets and maybe even on other life forms. You think about all of the aliens you have seen on television and in the movies. Is there life somewhere out there?

Suddenly a bright light races across the sky and then is gone. It lasted for only a second, but you are sure that you saw it. Maybe you even made a wish on that shooting star.

A moment later you see another, then another. You've seen shooting stars before, but you've

On a clear night, you can see countless fixed dots of light . . . and a few that sail through the sky.

never seen so many in such a short time. You watch as they zoom across the sky in all different directions. In just an hour, you have seen fifteen or twenty streaks of light dart across the star-filled sky.

As the lights race through the sky, questions race through your mind. What has caused this blizzard of "stars"? How can they move so fast? Why do they disappear so quickly? Are shooting stars somehow different from other stars?

A shooting star is different from other stars. In fact, a shooting star is not a star at all.

IT'S NOT A STAR

CHAPTER 2

How is a shooting star different from other stars?

The twinkling lights that you see shining in the night sky are suns. All suns, including the one that shines on our planet, are huge balls of fire. Most suns burn for millions and millions of years. Our sun has been burning for several billion years.

As suns burn, they produce heat and light. They give off so much light that you can see them from trillions of miles away. It would take a space-craft (that could fly over the United States in just 5 minutes) 82,500 years to travel to the closest star outside our solar system.

That streak of light that zooms across the sky and lasts only a second is actually a *meteor*, not a

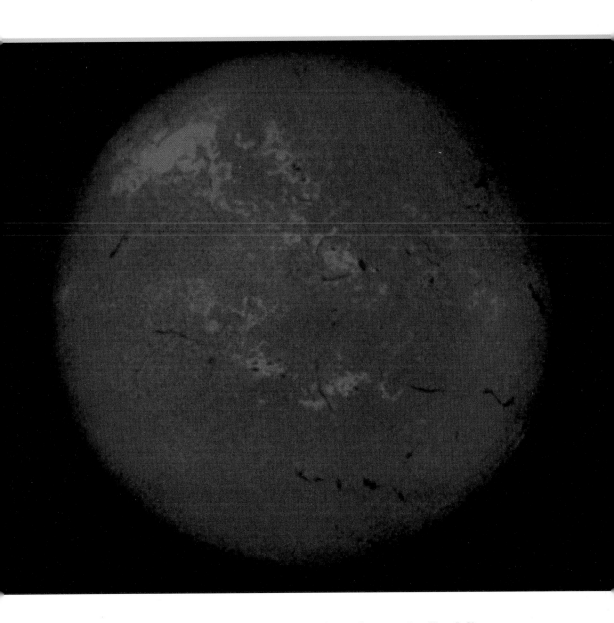

Our sun, like all other stars, is a huge ball of fire.

The Earth's atmosphere is the blanket of air that surrounds the planet (often protecting it from harmful objects and rays).

star. The light is produced when a dust particle or rock traveling through the solar system hits Earth's *atmosphere*, the blanket of air that covers Earth and contains clouds and winds.

Instead of being trillions of miles away, most meteors are less than 100 miles (160 km) away. A car can travel this distance in about 2 hours.

The dust particle or rock that causes a meteor is called a *meteoroid*. Like Earth and the other planets, a meteoroid travels around the sun in a fixed *orbit*. If a meteoroid's orbit intersects, or crosses, the Earth's *gravitational field*, it will be pulled toward Earth and collide with the upper atmosphere.

Why a Meteor Looks Like a Star

So if a meteor isn't a sun, why does it look like one?

Even the largest meteoroid is millions of times smaller than a sun. But when you see a meteor, it looks about the same size as a star. Why is this?

There are two reasons. First of all, objects that are farther away look smaller than objects that are close to you. Here's an example.

Imagine that you are at the top of a tall building. If you look down at the ground, you may see people walking on sidewalks or crossing the street.

Those people remind you of little ants scurrying from one place to another.

Even though you know those people are the same size as you, or maybe even bigger, they look very small when you are far away from them. The same thing happens when you look at the stars.

The second reason that a meteor looks like a star is because your eyes cannot see the details of objects that are very far away. The greater the distance, the less detail you can see.

You know that an old black Cadillac looks very different from a red convertible with the top down. But if you were in an airplane and looked at a group of cars traveling along a highway, you would not be able to tell which car was the Cadillac and which was the sports car. From that distance, all of the cars on the highway would look exactly the same.

To understand how your eyes can fool you by making things that are far away appear to be the same, pour some salt onto a table. Stand next to the table and look down at the salt. All of the grains of salt probably look pretty much the same. They look like a bunch of identical white specks. How could anyone possibly tell them apart?

Now move your head closer to the table and look at the salt again. When you examine the salt grains more closely, you'll realize that there's a lot

Although the meteor pictured here may appear to be about the same size as the stars, it's actually far smaller and closer.

more there than meets the distant eye! Those grains come in a tremendous variety of shapes and sizes. Some are two or three time bigger than others.

When you look at the night sky, almost all of the glowing lights up there appear to be the same size and distance from you. They're not. Even photographs taken through powerful telescopes cannot be used to accurately judge the size of stars or how far they are from Earth.

LOOK OUT, IT'S LEONID

At one time, people believed that shooting stars were caused by changes in the weather. The glowing trails of light seemed more closely related to lightning than to the stars that appear every night.

Scientists thought that whatever caused the meteors came from the clouds, just like rain and snow. In fact, the name meteor is actually a short-ened form of the word *meteorology*, which is the study of weather patterns. One night in 1833, scientists realized that meteors have nothing to do with the weather.

On the night of November 12, 1833, there was a breathtaking *meteor storm*. People all over North America were able to watch meteor after meteor

*During the Great Meteor Storm of 1833,
people came out of their houses to behold
as stars seemed to pour down from the sky.*

light up the sky. In Boston there were reports of 25,000 meteors per hour. It was like a silent fireworks display that lasted for 9 hours.

The Earth Spins, the Stars Don't

Nine hours is a long time. Think of all the changes that happen between 11:00 at night and 8:00 in the morning. At 11:00 at night, the sky is pitch black, except for the stars and maybe the moon. The world is quiet, and many people are asleep. At 8:00 in the morning, the sun is out, and you are probably getting ready to go to school.

The reason why it is dark outside at 11:00 at night and bright outside at 8:00 in the morning is because Earth *spins*. It is always spinning, from dawn until dusk and right through the night.

During the daytime, we are facing the sun. When it is night here, the sun is shining on the other side of Earth. When it's night in the United States, it's the middle of the day in China.

Has it ever seemed like a rain cloud was hanging right over your town, forcing you to play inside all day long? Clouds and smog can sit in one place for a long time. That's because they are carried right along with Earth as it spins, just like you are.

Everything in the atmosphere spins with Earth. Even though the moon orbits Earth, it does not spin along with Earth, and neither do the stars. You can see this for yourself.

On a clear night, go outside about an hour after dusk. Choose a star or constellation, such as the Big Dipper, that you will watch for several hours. Try to choose one that is fairly high in the sky. Make a drawing that shows the position of the star or constellation. Is it directly overhead? How far is it from the horizon?

After about two hours have passed, go outside and make another drawing that shows the position of the star or constellation that you are tracking. After another two hours have passed, go outside and make a third drawing.

Your drawings will show that the star or constellation has moved across the sky.

The stars rise and set, just like the sun.

A Meteor Storm Doesn't Spin

The scientists watching the meteor storm in 1883 were surprised when the *meteor radiant*, the point from which all of the the meteors emerged, moved across the sky along with the stars. They realized that the radiant spot was not spinning along with Earth. This meant that whatever causes meteors must come from outside Earth's atmosphere.

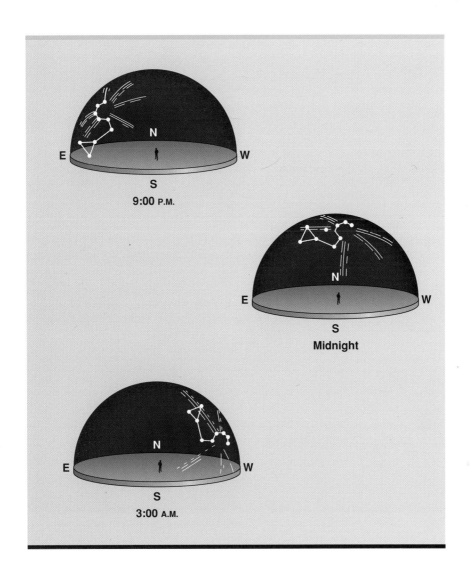

9:00 P.M.

Midnight

3:00 A.M.

All of the meteors in the Leonid meteor storm appear to emerge from the area within the constellation Leo.

*During the Leonid meteor storm,
swiftly darting streaks of light created the
"warp speed" effect often used in science
fiction shows and movies to create the illusion
of high-speed travel through space.*

Because the 1833 meteor storm was moving across the sky along with a constellation called Leo, it was named Leonid. By looking at historical papers, scientists discovered that a few Leonid meteors appear each year. However, the incredible Leonid *meteor shower* occurs only once every 33 years. The first report of the storm was made more than 1,000 years ago.

In 1966, people in Arizona described the Leonid meteor storm as a waterfall of stars. There were 100,000 meteors per hour! Some people said they felt like they were on a spaceship cruising into space at tremendous speed. The Leonid meteor storm is expected to be this spectacular on November 18, 1999. Will you be watching?

MAKING A METEOROID

CHAPTER 4

Meteors can be seen when a *meteoroid* collides with Earth's atmosphere. But where does a meteoroid come from?

Meteoroids are dust particles or rocks. Most are too small to see. If you notice a meteor that looks brighter than most stars, the meteoroid is probably about 1 inch (2.5 centimeters) or more across.

If you are lucky, you might spot a *fireball*. A fireball is caused by a meteoroid that is as big as a basketball. A meteoroid this large enters Earth's atmosphere about once in a century.

If a meteoroid larger than a basketball enters the atmosphere, it will explode noisily—as loudly as a bomb. If it is really huge, it may plunge straight through the atmosphere to the ground.

This "fireball" is caused by
a basketball-sized meteroid.

Comets, such as Biela, were created millions of years ago. Some complete orbits in less than 100 years. Others take more than 15,000 years to circle the sun once.

A Comet Disappears

Scientists think that most meteoroids come from *comets*. A comet is a small ball made of ice and rock. Comets were created billions of years ago, at the same time as Earth and the rest of the solar system. Like Earth, comets orbit the sun.

People first noticed the connection between meteors and comets in the late 1800s, when they observed some mysterious changes in a comet called Biela. Biela always passed close to Earth on its trip around the sun. During one trip, scientists noticed that Biela had split into two pieces. Clearly, this comet was starting to fall apart.

When the next date for Biela to pass by arrived, it didn't show up at all. Instead, people saw a meteor shower. This was the first clue that meteors must have something to do with a comet coming apart. Scientists now believe that they know exactly how a meteor is related to a comet.

When a comet gets close to the sun, the sun's heat causes some of the ice to evaporate. Small pieces of rock and dust particles are set free and become meteoroids.

Because Earth is close to the sun, you can see the trail of gas and dust left behind by the "head" of the comet as the ice evaporates. This trail is called the "tail" of the comet. Comet tails can be

As a comet ages, it breaks down into a series of pieces that continue to travel together. This picture shows different pieces of Comet Shoemaker-Levy 9 in orbit around Jupiter.

The trail of dust and gas that appears as a comet approaches the sun is called the tail, since it seems to follow the comet's main body.

anywhere from 50 to 100 million miles (80 to 160 million km) long.

The orbits of most comets is much larger than that of Earth or any of the other planets. While Earth circles the sun in 365 days, it may take as long as 500,000 years for a comet to orbit the sun once.

Since all comets have fixed orbits, scientists can easily predict where a comet will be at any given time. They can predict when they will be far away from Earth. They can predict when they will be near Earth. They can even predict when the meteoroids that come from comets will intersect with Earth's orbit.

Scientists know that Halley's Comet passes by Earth every 74 to 79 years. First observed more than 2,000 years ago, Halley's Comet most recently passed by Earth in 1986.

The meteor shower Eta Aquarid, which appears every year in early May, is believed to be caused by dust particles that have escaped from the head of Halley's Comet.

Asteroids Instead

Some meteoroids cannot be paired with a comet. For this reason, scientists believe that some meteoroids may come from another source—*asteroids*.

The band of asteroids between Mars and Jupiter is called the asteroid belt.

Asteroids are large chunks of rock that probably formed at the same time as the rest of the solar system. The largest asteroids have diameters of 620 miles (1,000 km).

Most asteroids can be found in an *asteroid belt* between Mars and Jupiter. These asteroids are relatively close together and often crash into one another. Meteoroids are formed when small pieces of rock break away from asteroids during collisions.

WARM WELCOME

When you dive into a swimming pool on a hot summer day, are you ever startled by the change? One instant you are soaring through the air. Your back and legs are warmed by the heat of the blazing summer sun. The noise of your friends' laughter and shouting fills your ears.

Then everything changes. Suddenly you're sinking through cool water that chills every inch of your flesh. As you slowly float toward the surface, you realize that you have entered a silent, blue world. If you think this is a big change, just imagine the change a meteoroid goes through as it sails into Earth's atmosphere.

Entering the Atmosphere

A meteoroid has an easy time traveling through space where there are few gases to get in its way. But moving through Earth's atmosphere is a different story. As the meteoroid travels through the gases that surround Earth, it rubs against all of the particles that make up the atmosphere.

To understand what happens when a meteoroid rubs against air particles, try rubbing your hand across your shirt very quickly. Do you feel the heat? That's because *friction*—another word for things rubbing together—causes heat. Friction causes meteoroids to get hot, too. And to glow.

Meteoroids begin to glow when they are between 80 and 50 miles (130 to 80 km) above Earth. As the meteoroid continues to plunge toward the Earth, it gets hotter and hotter until its temperature reaches about 4,000 degrees Fahrenheit (2,050°C). Most meteoroids are burned to a crisp before they are 20 miles (32 km) from Earth.

The Force of the Crash

Because the meteoroid is moving very fast when it crashes into the gases in the Earth's upper atmosphere, the *force* of the impact is great.

Think of an automobile crash in which a car accidently bumps another car parked in a parking

This meteor was photographed by campers in the Laguna Mountains in California.

lot. The moving car is probably traveling about 10 miles (16 km) per hour. Now think of a crash in which a race car collides with a wall at 200 miles (323 km) per hour. Which accident causes more damage?

The race car crash causes more damage because the car hits the wall with more force. The force is greater because the race car is moving faster.

The slowest meteoroids travel 10,000 times faster than a race car. The force of the impact between a meteoroid and the gases in the atmosphere is also thousands of times greater. The force of impact is so huge that light and heat are produced as the gases and the meteoroid break apart. The light you see flash across the night sky lasts until the meteoroid has been completely burned up.

Meteor Math

So how long does the average meteor last? Try to do the math. The answer will amaze you.

You know that a meteoroid is moving very fast when it enters Earth's atmosphere. Let's say it is moving about 25 miles per second (40 km/s). It starts to glow when it is 65 miles (105 km) above Earth and burns up when it is 40 miles (64 km) above the Earth.

If the glowing meteor plunged 25 miles (40 km)

at a speed of 25 miles per second (40 km/s), how long did it glow? That's right—for only about one second! So that fire in the sky that appears to be a star plunging to the Earth is really just a speck of dust that glows for about a second!

Sometimes a glowing meteor is left behind even after a meteoroid has burned up. This shining trail, which is visible for no more than a few minutes, is caused by the rapid heating of gases in the upper atmosphere.

Meteors Everywhere

Fortunately for lovers of meteor shows, meteoroids don't always travel alone. Sometimes, lots of meteoroids spray out from a comet. When many meteoroids enter Earth's atmosphere, each becomes a glowing meteor. The result is a breathtaking meteor shower.

Why is it called a shower? Because it's like the heavens are raining down sparks! A meteor storm is even more spectacular, and more rare, than a meteor shower. Sometimes, the meteors in a shower or storm look green, yellow, or even blue.

As you learned in Chapter 2, all of the meteors in a meteor storm or meteor shower seem to be coming from the exact same place in the sky. This spot is called the radiant. The 1833 meteor storm was

named Leonid because all of the meteors seemed to come from a point in the constellation Leo.

The meteors in a meteor shower do not really come from the exact same place in the sky, even though they are coming from the same comet. Once again, your eyes are playing tricks on you.

Have you ever looked down a long, straight highway? Did you notice that the dotted lines marking traffic lanes appear closer together in the distance? If you could see far enough ahead, those lines would appear to come from the same point.

It's the same with the paths of meteors. Even though they seem to come from the same point, they're really zooming through the sky in separate parallel lines.

During a meteor shower, the sky can actually look like it's raining stars.

JUST DROPPING IN

CHAPTER 6

KABOOOOOM!
A meteoroid that makes it all the way to Earth is called a *meteorite*. What do you think happens when a meteorite lands? Are hundreds of people crushed? Are dozens of buildings destroyed?

Actually, when most meteorites land, no one even notices. Most meteorites are tiny flakes of dust that didn't burn up as they fell toward Earth. Instead, they just floated down and settled onto the ground. There's another kind of meteorite, though, that's a lot less common—and a lot more scary.

Sometimes large meteoroids make it through Earth's atmosphere without burning up. Some are

This mixture of rock and iron is a visitor from space called a meteorite.

"Hey honey, it's not a volleyball!"
A man displays the 20-pound (9-kg) meteorite
that landed in his daughter's backyard.

made of rock, some are made of iron, and some are a mixture of rock and iron.

As you might imagine, scientists are thrilled to find these samples from space. Since these meteorites may have been formed at the same time that the planets were formed, scientists can study them for clues about what distant planets are made of. You can study these cosmic rocks, too, since many of them are on display in museums.

Megameteorites

In 1954, a woman in Sylacauga, Alabama, got a look at a meteorite that she wasn't expecting—from very close up. A meteorite fell right out of the sky, crashed through the roof of her house, and landed on her arm—leaving a bruise the size of a football. Luckily, a surprise visit from a meteorite this big is very rare.

But occasionally, meteorites can be even bigger. In 1908, a very large meteorite crashed down near Tunguska in Siberia. The impact caused entire forests to fall. Scientists have counted about 700 meteorite craters that are more than 0.6 miles (1 km) wide.

Can you imagine looking up at the sky and seeing a meteorite the size of a mountain headed your way? Scientists have calculated that a mete-

The enormous Tunguska meteorite landed with enough force to shatter an entire forest.

orite 1 mile (1.6 km) wide or bigger strikes Earth every several hundred million years. Since Earth has been around for billions of years, several of these meteorite mountains have probably struck our planet. And when they struck, they came down with more force than an earthquake or a volcano. They smashed into Earth with such power that they left huge craters that can still be seen today.

To get a sense of how powerful one of these crash landings can be, take a look at Meteor Crater in Arizona. Fifty thousand years ago a 300,000-ton meteorite struck this spot, leaving a *meteorite crater* 4,200 feet (1,280 m) wide. The crater's rim is as tall as a thirteen-story building.

That meteorite's landing sure made a big splash. It made solid ground splash up into the sky like water! What do you think it sounded like when this meteorite landed? How far away do you think the crash could have been heard, or seen, or felt?

Scientists believe that a gigantic meteorite crashing into Earth could transform life on the entire planet. As it landed, the meteorite could send enough dirt shooting up into the sky to create a cloud that would block out the sun.

With the sun blocked out, plants would die.

An immense meteorite can make a lasting impact on a planet's surface. Arizona's Meteor Crater was formed 50,000 years ago.

An Earth-sized fragment of comet Shoemaker-Levy 9 collided into Jupiter in 1992. Did this collision affect Jupiter the way a tremendous meteorite would affect Earth?

When plants die, animals that eat those plants would starve. If plant-eating animals died out, meat-eating animals that eat plant-eating animals would die out, too.

Scientists have recently located a huge crater in the Yucatan region of Mexico. This giant meteoroid's crash landing may have been responsible for killing the dinosaurs hundreds of millions of years ago.

Scientists hope to learn more about the effects that collisions of this kind can have by studying the effects of the recent collision of a comet called Shoemaker-Levy 9 on the planet Jupiter.

The Earth's Protective Shield

Don't worry! You don't need to start wearing a metal helmet to school. It will be a long, long time before another mountain-sized meteorite comes anywhere near our planet. Earth's atmosphere protects you from most meteors.

The moon, which has no atmosphere, is constantly bombarded with meteorites. With the help of high-powered telescopes, scientists have counted more than 3 billion meteorite craters larger than 3.3 feet (1 m) across on the surface of the moon.

*Since the moon has no atmosphere
to protect it from flying objects,
its surface is covered with craters.*

Safe beneath the atmosphere, we can marvel at the few mysterious rocks that have made it through. We can wonder at the meteor showers that light up the night sky. We can enjoy the silent beauty of stray visitors from the great beyond.

IS THIS A METEORITE?

CHAPTER 7

Is one of these visitors from space in your neighborhood, waiting to be discovered? What does a meteorite look like? Would you know one if you saw it?

If you come upon an unusual rocklike object, check it out. If your mystery object is made of *minerals*, such as quartz, pyrite, mica, or diamond, there's very little chance that it's a meteoroid. Meteoroids made of minerals are very rare. But if your mystery object is made of a *metal*, such as aluminum, lead, nickel, or iron, the chances that it came from space are much greater.

So test it with a magnet. If a magnet is attracted to your object, it just might be a meteoroid.

Unfortunately, most metallic rocklike masses

aren't from space. They're from factory furnaces. How can you tell if your mystery object was made in space? If it formed, in space, the object will

The intricate "Widmanstatten pattern," visible on the surface of this slab, indicates that it was formed in space.

have a special pattern on the inside. This pattern—called the *Widmanstatten pattern*—won't be found inside an object made in a furnace.

You shouldn't start trying to cut the object open to find the pattern though. Cutting the mystery object on your own could take a long time. It could also damage your mystery object. (And if it is a meteoroid, it should be treated with great care so it can be studied.) So take your mystery object to the nearest science museum or planetarium. There, an expert will make a tiny cut in the object and peek inside.

If the expert finds a Widmanstatten pattern, your mystery object really is a meteorite. Why is this pattern a dead giveaway that the object came from space?

Nickel and iron, the two metals that are found in most meteoroids, have slightly different weights on Earth. Since nickel is heavier than iron, when the two molten metals are mixed together on Earth, *gravity* pulls the nickel down below the iron. If a rock containing iron and nickel formed on Earth, the iron would be on one side of the rock and the nickel would be on the other.

In space there's no strong gravitational force acting on the metals—they're both weightless. So when they mix, they don't separate from each

This meteorite plunged right through the Donahue's ceiling, leaving the gaping hole in the ceiling pictured above.

other. Instead, they blend together in a striking jagged pattern. If the inside of your mystery object displays this striking pattern, you've come upon a visitor from space.

Or, who knows, maybe you'll get lucky and a meteoroid will come to you! While Robert and Wanda Donahue of Wethersfield, Connecticut, were watching TV in their livingroom, a 3-pound (1.4-kg) rock came crashing through the roof. No, the kids hadn't been playing basketball with a boulder. Tests revealed that the uninvited guest had come all the way from outer space. (Talk about dropping in unexpectedly!)

HOURS OF SHOWERS

CHAPTER 8

Would you like to see a meteor shower? You don't need a telescope, or even binoculars. But you do need patience. During most meteor showers, you can see forty to seventy meteors in an hour—that's only about one meteor per minute! So you might bring friends to make it more fun. And a radio to keep you awake.

The table below shows the best dates for catching meteor showers. All of these showers will be easier to see if you are away from city lights. It might be fun to bring a map of the constellations, so you can locate the constellation from which the shower will appear to come. But don't just watch any one part of the sky. The more sky you and your friends can keep an eye on, the greater your chance of spying meteors.

Meteor Shower	Best Date(s) for Viewing
Quadrantids	January 4
Lyrids	April 21 or 22
Eta Aquarids	May 3 or 4
Delta Aquarids	July 25–August 4
Perseids	August 11
Orionids	October 21
South Taurids	November 3–12
Leonids	November 17
Geminids	December 13
Ursids	December 22

GLOSSARY

asteroid—large chunks of rock that formed at the same time as the sun and planets.

asteroid belt—a large group of asteroids between Mars and Jupiter.

atmosphere—the layer of air and other gases that separates Earth from space.

comet—a small ball of ice and rock that orbits the sun.

fireball—the flash that you see in the sky when a meteoroid about the size of a basketball hits Earth's atmosphere.

force—a push or a pull.

friction—a force that resists the motion between

two objects or surfaces. If there is motion, energy is converted to heat.

gravitational field—the area surrounding a body, such as Earth, that is influenced by that body's gravity.

gravity—a force that pulls objects toward the surface of Earth.

metal—one type of chemical element (lead, aluminum, gold, iron, nickel).

meteor—the light that you see in the sky when a meteoroid enters Earth's atmosphere.

meteor radiant—the point from which all of the meteors in a meteor shower seem to emerge.

meteor shower—when a number of meteors appear at the same time (about ten or twenty per hour for several hours).

meteor storm—when many meteors appear at the same time (hundreds per hour).

meteorite—a meteoroid that hits the Earth.

meteorite crater—the hole formed when a very large meteoroid hits Earth.

meteoroid—a particle of dust or rock that enters Earth's atmosphere.

meteorology—the study of weather patterns.

mineral—a chemical compound that is not living (quartz, diamond, oil, sand, water).

orbit—to circle another body. The moon orbits Earth, and Earth orbits the sun.

spin—to turn.

Widmanstatten pattern—a pattern created by the mixing of iron and nickel when a rock forms in space.

FOR FURTHER READING

Asimov, Isaac. *Comets & Meteors*. New York: Dell. 1991.

Carlisle, Madelyn. *Let's Investigate Magical, Mysterious Meteorites*. New York: Barron, 1989.

Hamburg, Michael. *Astronomy Made Simple*. New York: Doubleday, 1993.

Pasachoff, Jay M. *Astronomy*. Peterson First Guides. New York: Houghton Mifflin,1988.

INTERNET RESOURCES

Comets and Meteor Showers
http://medicine.wysh.edu/kronkg/index.html

North American Meteor Network
http://medicine.wysh.edu/namn.html

INDEX

Page numbers in *italics* indicate illustrations.

ABOUT THE AUTHOR

Billy Aronson's other science books include two published by W. H. Freeman: *They Came from DNA*, which was named a NSTA/CBC Outstanding Science Book for Children in 1994, and *Scientific Goofs*, which has been printed in English, Chinese, and Turkish.

Billy's television writing credits include PBS's *Reading Rainbow* and *Where in Time Is Carmen Sandiego?*, CBS's *Really Wild Animals*, The History Channel's *Year by Year for Kids*, and MTV's *Beavis and Butt-Head,* as well as shows for Comedy Central, HBO, Nickelodeon, the Cartoon Network, and Children's Television Workshop. He is also a playwright, with a play featured in *Best American Short Plays 1992–93* (Applause Books).

Billy lives in Brooklyn with his wife, Lisa Vogel, and their children, Jake and Anna.